KALKATTA CHRONICLES

REAR-VIEW REFLECTIONS

SUPRIYA NEWAR

Best wishes.

Readomania

Readomania Publishing
A division of Kurious Kind Media Private Limited
466, DDA SFS Apartments, Pocket 1, Sector 22, Dwarka,
New Delhi – 110077
books.readomania.com
email: support@readomania.com
Facebook: facebook.com/iamreadomania
Twitter: twitter.com/iamreadomania

First Published in 2019 by Readomania

This is a work of creative nonfiction. The events are portrayed to the best of the author's memory. While all the stories in this book are true, some names and identifying details have been changed to protect the privacy of the people involved.

ISBN: 978-93-858542-1-7

Typeset in Palatino Linotype by Shine Graphics
Printed and bound at Thomson Press India Ltd.

Inside sketches by Sayan Chakraborty

Readomania

India has traditionally been the land of storytellers and a lot of us have an inherent skill of creating good plots, good stories and good narrations. With a little encouragement and support, many more authors will be widely read and attain a place in the sun. This is the essence of *Readomania*—an initiative that nurtures emerging stars of the literary world.

It would not be an exaggeration to say that *Readomania* is the talent hunt in fiction. It goes a step beyond by not just identifying the talent but also nurturing it and showcasing it to the world. In the process, we have created a powerhouse of content.

Readomania has four principal interest areas—traditional print publishing, online library of short stories and poetry, literary events and products.

The print publishing works towards delivering good quality content to the readers. We publish good authors in meaningful anthologies, novels and works of narrative non-fiction. Our books stand out for their perspectives, the plots, the language and most importantly their ability to enrich lives.

Take a break, read something nice, write something beautiful. Read our books or visit us at www.readomania.com and enjoy a whole new world of literature.

In memory of ...

My respected Dadi,
Late Smt. Rama Devi Newar

A humble tribute to her on behalf of
all her grandchildren.

&

My dear mother, Late Smt. Indu Newar

This one's for you, Maa.

&

Dedicated to an incorrigible, idiosyncratic yet
lovable chromosome called Calcutta.

Author's Note

Kalkatta Chronicles is about a world, a personal world of characters that were so deeply enmeshed, so regular in our daily lives that we noticed them only when they were absent or when they began to fade. These characters came in a wide range of encounters which included everyday habits, peculiar accents, odd signs, customs and traditions and of course people. But if one looked carefully, there was a somewhat subtle but common thread that ran across each of these characters.

Their story lay in hybrid; in mutation.

Kalkatta represents a slice of the city that had both wittingly and unwittingly borrowed from the British and the *Bhodrolok* but also could not help adding some of their own migrant seasoning to their borrowings, resulting in flavours that were completely fused and a social web that was gloriously entangled.

This Kalkatta had learnt to adopt and come to love *jhaal* and *jhol* and were past masters at managing *gondogol.* They called for a *chota* peg at clubs and were addressed by orderlies as *memsahib.* But there were hints of hybrid too: they opted for a *meetha-saada* paan that came to be known everywhere as Kalkatta *meetha,* beckoned their

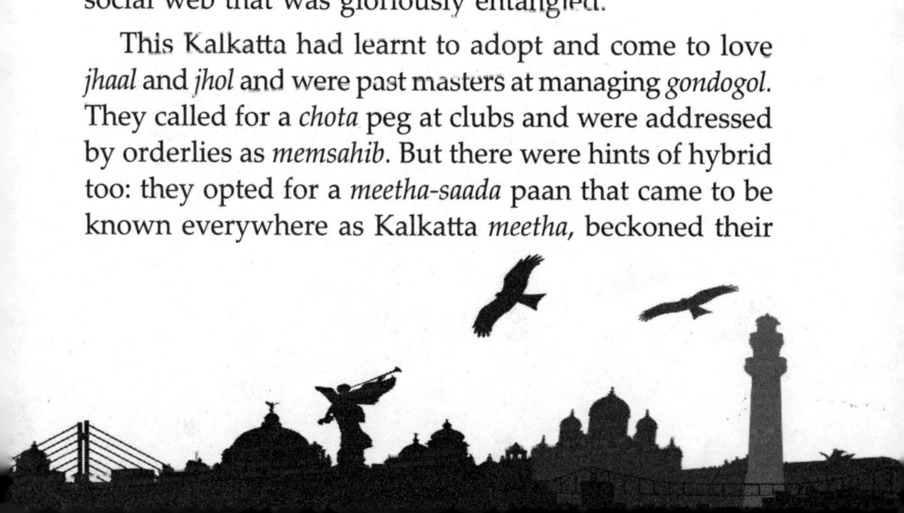

chauffeurs as *Driver ji* and referred to their female domestic help as *Ayah didi.* They went to schools that were English medium, convent or missionary, lived in *paras* but conversed with each other at home in Hindi and even Marwari.

Their's was a trilateral world that thrived in perpetual fusion.

Many of these nuances are now hard to find. With technology having seeped into our every breath, dissolving boundaries and identities like never before and instant being the only pace of time understood, many of them have faded into oblivion.

My idea here though, is not to lament change or indeed look at a world and an order gone by with rose-tinted glasses. Neither is it to compare one world with another. It is only to recall, share and reflect upon a microcosm that came into being by a collision of cultures; a world that often took the mundane, the ordinary to the extraordinary and created lasting impressions.

A microcosm called *Kalkatta.*

1

An Uplifting Ride

Its first master was a *dhoti*-clad, hardcore Rajput from Rajasthan who was respectfully addressed by all and sundry as *Thakar ji. Thakar ji* laid down the rules before passing on the baton to Bhogiram, a Bihari with a booming voice and formidable whiskers. Bhogiram ran the show for a good decade before handing over the baton to young Raju.

The baton in question was a key—a key without which the running and faculties of our perpetually in motion, multi-storeyed household stood grounded.

In an age when automatic elevators had not come into being, it was this key, which was a magic lever with the power to command an uplifting ride.

A solid, large, handle-like device, the key had to be plugged in or out of the main socket and turned in a particular way to set the cage in motion.

The elevator was reduced to nothing more than an open, wooden cage without this heavy, brass key. There was a staircase of course which one could take and rise manually and the habitants of the first floor often did so. But being lodged on the third floor of a tall building made the staircase a long and laborious option for us; one that left most of our portly elders huffing and puffing. The younger members, though physically able, were discouraged to take it unescorted as the all-black staircase often ran into dark and dingy corners.

What all of this meant was that the 'lift' as it was more commonly referred to then, was a prized ride and each of its masters, the many 'liftmen' no less than prized jockeys.

These jockeys had some unwritten rules about lift usage that were followed by one and all, quite unquestioningly. Lifts were used only for the uphill ride; while descending, everybody was expected to take the stairs other than in extraordinary circumstances. One such circumstance was if any of the families was going for a vacation. The lift would then have to be called up to ferry the luggage down. In no time, this breaking news would spread to every corner of the building with complete details, the liftman, often playing the role of chief reporter.

The other more worrisome circumstance used to be the coming over of guests, especially during festivals or special occasions. In fact the guests would habitually check the availability of both the lift as well as the family members prior to scheduling their appointment. At times, when the lift reported an 'out of order' condition, appointments were calmly rescheduled. Since all the families living at every end of the building were Marwaris, their festivals and occasions too tended to fall at the same time, leading to surge hours for the liftman.

Interestingly, the pecking order of the guests could be determined by which ones took the stairs down and which ones were escorted downstairs in the lift.

As soon as the courtesy visit of important guests neared its end, we would get together and collectively start hollering, *'liffffftt, liffffftt'* signalling the liftman, to bring his beloved up to our floor. Sometimes the holler would work; at other times, a servant had to scoot down, find the absconding rogue and get him to bring the lift up. On any given day, the liftman customarily made himself unavailable at least a couple of times. When he did the Houdini, he would do so with his key, which he was rather possessive about, leaving only a sickly cardboard sign that read 'Out of Order' hanging from the lift as a missive. Therefore, on days when the family needed to make an impression, he had to be forewarned not to do so and for abundant precaution his pockets were left gently padded to prevent him from doing an ill-timed vanishing act.

Never once though, were guests or visitors ever asked which floor they needed to go to. The liftman had a tremendous memory for every face and would intuitively be able to match the guests to their respective floors and units. Most guests were known to him of course. Even if they weren't, he had the horse sense to dole out a *salaam* to the right one when he anticipated a *bakshish* that was likely to come his way. Passengers, who showed any nerves while taking the thudding ride up, would be duly placated by the liftman who assured them of their safety.

The one time we encountered him daily, was when each of us would return from school. The timing would often coincide with his siesta hour and his mood would range from being indifferent to grumpy. The lift had three brass rods along its inside periphery, upon which we loved to climb, rest our haunches or at least our school bags and water bottles. There were days when this irked him and he would scold us, asking us not to jump around in the lift. On other days, he would just sit quietly on his wooden stool which by then had acquired an impression of his rear end and was placed next to the key and merely operate the lift. Only on days, when our tomfoolery was entirely missing, did he enquire about our well-being and asked us if everything was okay. *'Iskool mein kya hua? Parikcha tha kya?'*

But his kindly side was usually short-lived and we quickly found reason to fight with each other again. A perpetual bone of contention would be our very serious game of cricket getting aborted every time our rubber ball took a big hit and landed right in the pit of the lift.

Unlike today's elevators, these very stately looking lifts stood parked a little above their base level. The two-feet-odd cavity thus created would often swallow our ball, bringing our games to an abrupt halt. No sooner did this happen, that our negotiations began. We would plead with him to raise the lift just a bit, so that one of us could slip in through the gap and retrieve the ball. More often than not, our request was not entertained. But on the odd occasion that he did relent, we would land up excavating the treasure of half a dozen rubber balls lying buried in various stages of decay and deflamation.

Once in a very rare while, he would allow us to operate the lift under his strict supervision of course. Just being able to touch and hold the magic key would set our nerves tingling. At other times, the liftman would show off his prowess by bringing the lift to a stop, even in between floors, just by adjusting the lever. The lift would obey his orders and jerk to a halt.

The other faithful companion of the lift was the daily ritual of *load shedding*. What exactly was the load and how its shedding would punctually coincide with dusk remained a mystery. Just when evenings set in, the load would shed, leaving the lift grounded and lifeless; its gate ajar, its chamber dark and abandoned. The breadwinners of every family who would start returning home soon after, would utter a curse or two and grudgingly start trekking up, leaving their briefcases and large steel tiffin carriers behind to be lugged up by their respective drivers.

Hanuman Chalisas were resorted to when the lift shuddered and came to a grinding halt in the middle of a ride. This could happen either due to a sudden power cut or a mechanical failure. Unlike modern contraptions however, these lifts had collapsible gates that once opened, allowed the passenger to interface with the world outside. To that extent, one was relieved of feeling utterly suffocated or entrapped. An alternate DC (direct current) line had to be switched on for the lift to complete its ride after which it stood still, until the conditions were more conducive.

Sometimes around Diwali or in case of a windfall gain, the lift would get a face lift. Its wooden body and its brass fixtures would be given a polish; the large mirrors that took up its inside walls rubbed until squeaky clean, allowing the guests who boarded it to get a perfect reflection; its rickety iron fan that created more noise than it dissipated air, freed of cobwebs. On such occasions, the liftman too sat up straighter and prouder on his designated stool donning his newly stitched, ironed and monogrammed uniform.

By the late 70s, large Marwari families had begun to disintegrate and move into ample bungalows and modern apartments in the central and southern parts of the city, abandoning the old fashioned northern fringes.

Many of the lift's once regular passengers are now no more. Many others are no longer visitors. But even today, every now and then, there comes along a visitor who once aboard, can't help feeling quite amazed by this signature and very uplifting ride.

2

Bespoke

His were the only eyes that stayed laced with *surma* and his was the only ebony face in our firmament that had a pruned salt and pepper, prickly beard stuck to it.

Of the five floors on each side of the courtyard or *chowk* around which numerous families resided and of the regular stream of incessant guests, visitors and stray footfalls all put together, his was a name and face that distinctly stood out. For his name was Iqbal. He was the family's bespoke tailor. To be precise, the bespoke 'gent's' tailor.

The once unputdownable *safas* or headgear that were signature male attire for the entire community had long been put down and were now reserved for weddings only. *Dhotis* too had been tucked away in exchange for trousers or *patloons.* With adaptability being their hallmark, the community had instinctively understood that if they had to conduct business with the *bhadrolok,* they would be better off giving up their wardrobe angularities.

The menfolk had therefore come to don trousers and shirts for daily wear. Sometimes when business meetings with General Managers of large PSUs beckoned, they would even deck up their shirts with ties. Not all of them however had learnt to knot their ties perfectly, but true to their wont, had found a solution for the same. At least two loosely knotted ties would stay hanging on the inside door of almirahs, ready to be hung around the neck and tightened on demand.

Ready-to-wear shirts, trousers or suits were not the order of the day. They were neither in vogue nor commanded an iota of respect. Repeating a shirt or suit was no crime but donning something pre-fabricated was unheard of. Even daily office wear shirts and trousers were made to order for each male in the family. And since the male species of the clan came in a variety of age groups, sizes and shapes, the cloth had to be cut differently for each.

Iqbal did the honours for decades.

Generally turning up on Sunday afternoons, sans any knock on the door he would confidently stride into each room to perform his duty. He had long dispensed with a 'May I come in'. Not that a knock on the door was even possible, for all doors of all rooms were statutorily left open, with only a fluttering full-length curtain providing an apology of a privacy. Literally speaking, there was no room for privacy nor was the concept either understood or entertained. Closed doors during the day spelt trouble or indicated that sensitive issues such as marriage proposals or money matters were being discussed.

Besides, Iqbal had wound his way to the precincts of our traditional Marwari set-up through a community reference that was above question, giving him the diplomatic immunity to saunter in.

Armed with his heavy, chiselled pair of scissors that looked ready to strike and garlanded by his inch tape dangling down his neck, he would give any pleasantries a miss and get down straight to business. The task at hand varied from either taking a measurement for a new order or delivering an order taken previously.

Now, new orders were not a problem. Unplucking a short blunt pencil that stayed tucked around his ears, he would take down meticulous notes in Urdu, in a rag of a diary that he carried in a plastic packet. He only sounded grunts and utterances; full sentences from him were rare. Alongside, he would make little marks on the provided fabric, often purchased from Akbarally's, with a morsel of a blue chalk that stayed locked in the diary. He missed nothing: the collar, the sleeve, the length, the cut, the angle, the pockets, the cummerbund, the *chudi, et al*. Regular orders ranged from simple *kurta-pajamas, churidars,* shirts, sorry 'bush shirts' to trousers and sometimes even uniforms for the young school-going boys. But come the wedding season and his assignments would change to formal wear such as safari suits, sports coats, Nehru jackets, *sherwanis, bandhgalas* and so on. Sometimes, a precious sample, procured from the reigning Joneses of the society would be shown to him as reference to be copied in toto.

Often, these would come with very tight deadlines, for generally the men would agree to a new pair of threads only after much insistence from their better halves. With the brief given, the material and a token advance collected for the job, Iqbal would take his leave, promising to come back on a stipulated date.

Now would begin the waiting for Godot because though the stipulated date came and went, there would be no sign of Iqbal. Worry signs, though did begin to appear causing tempers to fly high. The wives accused the husbands of being lazy and leaving things for the last minute. More concerned about orders, tenders and cash flow management, the husbands of course did not take any of their reproaches too seriously.

With no means to track down the tailor or follow up on the bespoke merchandise, the wives, each one a skilled seamstress, would begin working on Plan B that entailed pulling out the previous season's clothes from large iron trunks and drying them in the sun to let the moth ball odour out. Sometimes, while sitting together in the sultry afternoons, repairing a button hole or a hanging trouser loop, the womenfolk would discuss the impending doom. None of this particularly flustered the men who had left the department of fashion to be dealt with exclusively by the women.

Just the night before the grand date when the family would have sat down for yet another candlelit dinner, thanks to the regular feature of load shedding, a ray of light would come filtering through. Iqbal, in his standard loosely fitted, stark white *kurta-pajama* would cut through the all pervading gloom like a beacon of hope, as he made his entry with two very promising looking brown paper bundles tied up with strings. With a desperate apology and a half-baked excuse, he would tear open the bundles, choosing not to pay any attention to the mouthful that would parallelly be served to him. Instead, he would try to entice with his goods and craftsmanship.

This time around, the men would get flustered. For whilst trying out the new clothes, if they pointed out any discomfort in the fitting, complained of a crease or a pleat not falling into place or a collar not sitting right, Iqbal wouldn't accept any of it. He would belt out one explanation after the other, tugging at a corner, stretching the fabric, blaming it on the light, assuring it would fall into place after ironing and so on. A devout Muslim, he swore on his Lord, that the 'fitting' was perfect. Most of the times, his word would be the last one. It was only on rare occasions that his argument and perseverance did not win and his tailoring needed re-doing, a service that he would grudgingly provide.

I'm not sure what made him a success across the family for years together, for he wasn't necessarily the finest tailor around. Was it the sheer laziness on the part of the menfolk to step out and deal with unfamiliar territory? Was it the mutual ease of payment and credit that both parties trusted each other with? Or was it the silent rapport that he enjoyed with each of his esteemed customers (and their better halves)? Whatever may have been the secret of the arrangement, each party had got used to the other and in the process, Iqbal, who never so much as had more than a glass of water at our household, became a bespoke family heirloom.

In fact, to my sheer delight and amazement a few years ago, when my sister, many shores away, wanted a *sherwani* to be stitched for her son who was groom to be, she could think of none other than Iqbal. The job was finally carried out when his number was sourced and a phone call was made to Iqbal's protégé and son, Bilal who was more than happy to oblige. The *sherwani* turned out to be truly bespoke. The groom then is now a young father; my sister a beaming grandmother.

Evidently, his pair of bespoke scissors had ripped through more than just the many layers of fabric. It had ripped through the layers of time.

NOTE BOOK
GEOGRAPHY
GUM

3

Brown Paper Clothing

I'm given to understand that they now come prefabricated in transparent, highly durable sheets, complete with labels *et al*, that are designed to last through the year.

Some others have gone green with the wrapping coming in paper that proudly proclaims its recycled status in keeping with today's carbon footprint-conscious generation.

No fuss. No mess.

It has become quite a simple off-the-shelf purchase, the convenience and efficiency of which has led to the once annual ritual of brown paper clothing becoming fairly null and void.

The ritual would be much the same every year. Since many of us went to similar kinds of schools,

the new academic sessions for all of us would begin at similar points in time too. But it was only towards the fag end of the holiday that sometimes felt a tad long while it was on but a trifle short when it was close to getting over, that it would dawn upon us to start preparing for our new class.

Since hardly any of us had any homework to deal with barring the odd essay on 'How did you spend your summer holidays' and tuitions were unheard of, the only real preparation was to get our books for the next academic year in order.

Procuring the textbooks wasn't much of a deal. Most of the times we were meant to use second-hand textbooks that had been carefully preserved after their first run with an older sibling, a cousin or even a distant acquaintance. In case the textbooks weren't available within the network, one would only have to hop over to College Street aboard an L-9, for a second-hand copy and invariably come out triumphant.

The idea of purchasing textbooks was considered only when there was a change in the prescribed text or the one available for use was particularly tattered.

When we did purchase textbooks, there were only one or two prescribed shops we would go to. For all the girls in the family, there was a hole in a Park Street wall called Metropolitan Book Company. It was almost like a clandestine slit through which one slipped in a sheet where the list of required books was noted down. Many years later, I discovered similar slits at liquor shops, through which I dared to put in very different requisitions! There would be a standard question from the grouchy salesman, 'Modern? *Kon* class?' Modern meant Modern High School. Once he knew which class, he would pull out the entire set effortlessly as the list hadn't changed in years and he knew it by heart. If the purchase was sizeable or if he was feeling generous, he would throw in a sheet of labels, free of charge.

Carefully clutching the precious packet, we would head back home.

Once home, the packet would be torn open hungrily. It was a bewildering matter how the very books that would torment me through the year with their fractions, prepositions, maps and graphs could be a source of such joy at the beginning of our acquaintanceship.

My father who just about knew which class I was being promoted to and wasn't really concerned with things like grades or marks, always leapt out for the Hindi poetry book, *Padya Bharti.* With great relish, he would fold the book to a poem by Jaishankar Prasad or Maithili Sharan Gupt and start reciting it loudly drowning out my cries of warnings that the spine of my already fragile text book was getting further compromised.

His recital provided the background score to the next step of the ritual—a statutory inspection of the purchase of the day. My brothers, who were only a few years older to me, would look at the Mathematics books and sagely tell me to practise hard. At least one of them would pick up a 'K.C. Nag', look at the algebra equations and discard them as child's play. Another one would state wisely, 'Remember, in Physics, everything is about the how!' Leafing through the history books, they would get into an argument over the correct pronunciation of 'Renaissance', each one having a different opinion about which letter in the word was meant to be silent.

The new lot of books would be kept alongside the already sourced older books that required tender mending. But my favourite pile was that of the shiny, gleaming exercise books, all in mint condition, some ruled some otherwise, waiting to be inked. That in a matter of just a few months, many of them would have ugly red scars was a tragedy I chose not to worry about.

I would call it a day by fastidiously stacking my precious stuff in a safe corner and putting it all away along with a roll of tape, a pair of scissors, a bottle of glue and sheets of labels. The next day was a big one, as these babies would be readied for the year ahead. But the interval would be long, for it was only after the womenfolk were done with their more routine chores and what seemed like an eternally long wait, did they get down to the heaps of books waiting to be clothed.

Reams of brown paper ranging from shades of mahogany to teak were soon ripped and slashed to suit the covers of different books. My aunts and my mother were past masters at the job. I wondered if they ever felt bad for having been denied the opportunity to consume the very textbooks they clothed for so many of us, year after year. Even if they did, they kept it to themselves, perhaps sanguine in the fact that what had been denied to them was being made available to us.

The task was carried out quite gaily with *Vividh Bharti* providing background music or a pocket transistor belting out some cricket commentary in Hindi... *'aur khoobusrati se long on ke aage se jaati hui, gend boundary line par'*.

First, the books were strategically placed on sheets of brown paper to be cut in a way that ensured minimum wastage. Once this was done, the protruding ends of the paper would be deftly folded into the front and back covers, edges smoothened out and cello tape slapped on for support in case of particularly heavy or large books. I played a key role in the adhesive department. Holding the cello tape roll around my thumb I would cut small pieces and keep them taped to the edge of my finger tips so that they were ready to be peeled off and applied on demand.

Next came the 'second-hand' books that needed a delicate makeover. This operation began by taking off their worn-out covers, clothing them with a fresh brown paper sheet and gently mending their frayed edges with tape. Post the makeover even these textbooks matched the newly purchased ones, at least cover for cover.

Their insides were a different story. These already consumed texts came with their own advantages. Despite my hold over Arithmetic and other 'Science subjects' not really being enviable, I could easily gather the answer to the problem posed as it would often lay inscribed on the page in faded pencil. The only remaining problem for me was to arrive at the answer already at hand!

The Biology books sometimes had pencil doodles which I often failed to decipher but which some girls in class had a devilish giggle about. By the time we reached secondary school, textbooks also carried numerous compatibility results between the oddest pairs, arrived at through the very scientific process of 'FLAME'!

Once the operation was complete, the entire lot would be buried under some flat, heavy object that varied from being tomes like the *Encyclopaedia Britannica* to the family harmonium that was made to sit on the pile of books overnight to flatten them out and get them attuned for use. If the pile was too large, they would be tucked under a mattress that sat directly on the floor and the combined weight of the family would be put to good use to set the covers in, well and proper.

The next day, the large pile of freshly clothed books would be retrieved from down under their respective burial points. After a round of inspection, they were now ready for their final dressing: labels that had to be glued on, using the thick glue from stinky blue bottles that had to be applied by a brush attached to the cap of the bottle. Glue sticks or stick-on labels were still in the future. Customarily, at least a couple of labels would get glued on either upside down, on the wrong side or even on the wrong book. After the labels were dry, our names would be carefully penned on each and the books had now officially found owners, at least for that year. Sometimes, to my delight, I was also allowed to inscribe the labels on my own, a privilege I carried out very carefully after filling up my fountain pen with Royal blue Chelpark ink.

Quick fixes and ready-to-go being the order of the day, I suppose much of this would hardly be feasible any more. The very idea would be scoffed at as being a waste of time and energy. Why opt for a long winded route in the age of smart? But then there was something about this and many such ordinary activities that were long drawn enough to offer time and space for the creation of memories and for the involvement of many at once. Perhaps which is why, even though the colour may have long since gone pallid, brown paper clothing remains golden.

4

Let There Be Light

It seems when God said, 'Let there be light', we weren't paying even the slightest attention. Or perhaps our daily routines and retinas were so well adjusted to the darkness that we missed out on the prophecy. Only our darkness went by a unique name and was a phenomenon unbeknown to most other cities.

We called it load shedding.

For more than one and a half decades, the entire city faced hours of power cuts at various points of time in the day, every day. While other places chose to term it as a power cut, Calcutta being Calcutta had to have a more charming term for it and called it load shedding, implying something was clearly overloaded and it needed shedding.

Load shedding was as confirmed in our daily lives as the sun coming up. So we had taken it to be most natural and had learnt how to be accommodative. If Delhi had its hot summer loo and Bombay its monsoon downpour, then we had our load shedding. The shedding of the load took place in a rather disciplined pattern. There were neighbourhoods that had load shedding in the afternoons and others that had load shedding in the evenings. There were months when we knew it would be a post-dinner affair and others when one would wake up bathed in sweat. But unless the pattern was severely broken or the load shedding hours became unbearably long, no one really questioned it. It was after all a huge leveller in society; a phenomenon that affected the entire order—you could be a *babu* or a *seth,* a Commi or a Capi, but candles were part of your monthly ration.

Only the wax differed.

Growing up in these less loaded times had their own advantages. We generally fell in the evening slot which meant that just after dusk our home would be plunged into darkness. In fact, since it went neighbourhood wise, the shedding would affect not just a single building but an entire locality leaving it bereft of electricity.

It gave us the perfect excuse to skip studies and homework. Maps and graphs were not even attempted. Of course, our excuses would be decimated and we were ticked off by the same answer each time. *'Kya hua batti nahi hae to? Vidyasagar ji toh street light mein padhte the. Tum log ko to pehle suvidha chahiye.'* (How does it matter if there's no electricity? Vidyasagar studied under a streetlamp. You all demand too many privileges!)

With the lights gone and the air sticky with humidity, our verandas became our chief hangout zone. Luckily, every single room came with an attached veranda. Southward open, all of them looked out into the main road while some even received a wonderful breeze. The one attached to my grandmother's room was where the women gathered, that is if they had finished attending to their kitchen chores. Folding fans in hand, they took turns to rustle up the breeze while sharing all kinds of sundry gossip. Another one was more the male domain where the discussions revolved around numbers and yet another where my uncles secretly smoked.

The veranda where we congregated and sat for hours was the one adjoining our drawing room or *gaddi*. It was our informal extracurricular activity as well as *adda* zone. The breeze would be too much for any candle to survive and the only light we received was either from the moon or from the reflection of a serpentine queue of traffic tail lights shining brighter in the dark; quite suitable for shadow art on the walls. It was in this veranda that we played *antakshari* or recited poetry or even quizzed each other or random trivia. Cricket scores and games would be discussed and dialogues from *Sholay* and all Amitabh Bachchan films delivered over and over again. Evening after evening would be spent playing dumb charades, though it was much later that I came to know the correct spelling and the meaning of the word 'charade'.

On days when we were privileged enough to get a hurricane lamp, board games were laid out—Spellcraft, Monopoly, Chinese Checkers, Dominoes, Close Up, Chess and Ludo. Sometimes on weekends, the elders joined us in our play and we would have fabulous sessions of *Chaupad,* the game made famous by Shakuni *Mama* in the *Mahabharat*. We'd see a fascinating role reversal as elders got excited like children, rolling out the dice, plotting victory over other contenders.

If sessions at the veranda started getting monotonous, then there was always the game of dark room—essentially hide and seek in the dark. A building that offered a variety of nooks and crannies and remained plunged in darkness for hours was ideal for playing dark room. Sometimes, while hiding in the dark, we would gather embarrassing family gossip which we didn't know how to process. At other times, the darkness frightened us, making us keener to be found than to remain in hiding.

Men had an advantage over women when it came to coping with the load shedding. They would disrobe and be at ease in their vests almost as soon as the lights went out. Our cook, a Brahmin *maharaj,* would be bare bodied barring his sacred *janeu* and *dhoti,* as he lit the *choolah.* The women however, would have to continue to be draped in nine yards, sometimes, with their saree *pallu* stretched to cover their heads as a mark of respect to the elders, the ends of which they tugged at to wipe their sweaty faces.

The aura around load shedding was different at different times of the day and the year. In the summers, no power in the mornings meant three generations learning how to wake up and kick start the day early. The kitchen would swing into action the earliest as did the queues for morning ablutions. One of the other reasons prompting it was that long hours of load shedding meant the pumps not working, leading to a perpetual water shortage and the water in the taps reducing to a trickle in no time. At any point in time, there was a ready assortment of buckets and tumblers filled with water. After all, a business family knew it was important to save for a dry day.

Afternoons would be sultry and quieter, marked by typical street calls and cries of *sil katao,* the rickshaw puller's bell, the *dhuniya* tugging at his string or a mini bus conductor, slapping the body of the bus, chanting his route: '*Shyambajar, Sovabajar, Bagbajar, Chitpur, Paikpara; khali...khali....*' Women rested in their respective rooms, a maid servant fanning them gently, partly dozing off herself.

Come rains and we waited with bated breath for the *kal boisakhi* or the Nor'westers to lash in every evening as we ran out despite protesting mothers to the terrace to enjoy the wild breeze and the celestial drama in the sky.

Sound of every kind acquired a heightened dimension in the dark. Every sneeze and snort, every spoken word and thought seemed to echo louder. The neighbourhood *kirtan* accompanied by the *manjira* performed across the street, the evening *aarti* with the ringing of the conch shell in tandem with the tram car's distant bell, together cast a unique spell. Early morning's slumber would often be broken by the cries of '*Ram naam satya hae...*', since we fell on the route of the final journey to Nimtallah Ghat.

While the entire place was lit mostly by candles, kerosene lamps were lit and placed at strategic points for a slightly higher voltage. Filling these lamps with *mitti ka tel* was a daily task performed by a designated help. At many spots, candles could be found shoulder to shoulder with kerosene lamps, the risk of a fire breaking out not perhaps bothering anyone too much. The burning candles would leave a sort of permanent mark on the mosaic flooring all along the corridor. Actually, they were purposelessly left glued to the ground in at least two spots in every room, the melting wax sliding down their white bodies and settling in a heap at their roots. We would compete with each other at heroically running our fingers through the burning flame and coming out unscathed.

Battery operated devices were well in vogue and almost everyone had bulky steel-bodied torches filled with large batteries to get through any critical work during the unlit hours. There would also be the odd transistor that would run on batteries. It was however used somewhat sparingly and made to run at a stretch only on days when a crucial test match was on. Sometimes, when two such transistors were in operation, they were placed in such a way that the entire house resonated with the commentary of Garry Sobers or Richie Benaud. On other days, Ameen Sayani with his *Geetmala* would fill our prime time. Inverters that were rudimentary contraptions made out of car batteries could also be found, though their state of health ranged from hardly working to not at all. They could not match the might of load shedding and after powering a tube light or two rather sickly, would die out themselves.

Miraculously, however, there were some specific days in the year when the load would never shed. Four such sure shot days would be during the Durga Puja festival, when the entire city would get additional power, clearly through some divine intervention and stay glittering and lit. With all schools and offices being totally shut, we would make the most of those days, gallivanting from *pandal* to *pandal,* night after night. Diwali was however a different story, as the load would never fail to shed exactly when it was time for the rituals and prayers, provoking at least one member to remark that Diwali meant little in this city.

Much later, gensets or mini generators came to be commonly found in homes. Fuelled by petrol and more powerful than invertors, we tolerated their blare as they could fight the load shedding at least for a few hours.

Nothing however matched the joy and ejaculation as when the lights came back on and the fans acquired life again. We would race each other to blow out the lit candles with a big whoosh amidst collective cries of *'light aa gaya'!*

SHOLAY

5

Matinee Magic

At a time when electronic entertainment was limited to Doordarshan and Akashvani with most of the transmission remaining largely dependent on the health of the ever fragile antennas, Hindi cinemas played a great role and reigned over our entertainment quota almost single-handedly.

The family could be tackling any number of issues—from everyday household matters to *bandhs and hartals,* knee-deep waterlogged roads or dry taps, tenders, quotations and ebbing cash flows to an absentee cook—whatever the woe, Hindi cinema was the great collective escape that managed to put each member out of his or her misery. At least for a bit.

Though going to the cinemas was a regular affair, it was not an ordinary one. There was much thought and planning that went into going for a movie. After all, the age of *Permit Raj* was one where everything from money, time and individual independence came statutorily rationed. Therefore, even if the tickets could be afforded, one had to deal a fair hand and take turns so that everyone else in the family got their due chance to go for a 'picture'. As a rule, night shows were not permitted, thereby limiting the options to either a noon or a matinee. With elders setting the precedent of 'early to bed, early to rise', going for a night show was stepping out of the *Lakshman rekha* and came with strict reprimand.

The *bahus* were particularly careful of not landing up for the same show as their various in-laws. Catching and enjoying an onscreen romance or worse a cabaret number together was an embarrassment that was deftly avoided at all costs. Besides, the movie theatre was one of the very few opportunities that afforded couples any privacy with each other during waking hours.

Sunday mornings after breakfast was generally reserved for hours of free-wheeling *adda* where all kinds of neighbours and relatives casually poured in and out. The subject of Hindi cinema ritually cropped up amidst other discussions with Radio Ceylon or *Binaca Geetmala* simultaneously doling out chartbusters from the prized Murphy radio set. These songs as I was to realise later had caused a deep dent in me and were primarily responsible for kick starting a tremendous love for music.

Film magazines were seen as frivolous purchases as well as confirmed injurious to the health of family values. They were hard to come by other than dated ones at beauty parlours and dentists' chambers, pages of which were quickly ripped out to be later neatly pasted on the insides of Godrej almirahs. The decision to go for a new release or to skip it therefore largely depended on the matinee gossip gathered by word of mouth.

Though almost everyone loved the silver screen and had their own matinee idols, the family had two distinct camps when it came to choosing a film. There was a camp which enjoyed movies that conveyed a social message. This camp eagerly consumed banners such as RK Films and Bimal Roy Productions that had unapologetic socialist overtones and came out puffy eyed but happy after watching films like *Sujata, Bandini, Shree 420, Do Aankhen Baarah Haath, Jagriti* and so on. Women of this camp never forgot to pack extra handkerchiefs in their clutches.

The second camp however, was not particularly interested in coping with *'rona dhona'* in films. Dealing with their own everyday realities was quite enough for them and they didn't care for realities being accentuated on the silver screen. For them, films meant songs shot in Kashmir, Ooty and Nainital and confirmed happy endings, dotted with song and dance and dramatic ups and downs.

Too young to have our own likes and dislikes and accepted by both camps, some of us landed up sampling the entire platter: the sensitive Balraj Sahni, the eloquent Dilip Kumar, the suave Dev Anand, the irrepressible Shammi Kapoor, the angry young man, Amitabh Bachchan and everyone else who came in between.

But there was a monumental task one had to fulfil before one could occupy a precious seat in the hallowed Dress Circle of a theatre—the task of procuring cinema tickets.

More often than not, the tickets had to be purchased in black as the box office would be declared 'house full' within only a few minutes of the counter opening. In reality, the DC or the dress circle and balcony tickets would get bought out by a handful of touts who later sold them at an *'ek ka teen'* or one for the price of three each. These touts could be found loitering around box offices and had a fixed clientele. Hawk-eyed, they would duly acknowledge each *babu* and *memsahib* and come up to the car with appropriate goods: pink and green shreds of paper with seat numbers scribbled in dark lead that had the power to command *khul ja sim sim* and open up the gateway to proscenium theatres.

Though the deal was always laced with negotiations on both sides, the touts had become experts at reading their customer's psychology and they knew exactly when to extract maximum value and when to relent. Since their wares also came with short expiry dates, they allowed their customers to have the last word. The touts also acted as cine guides. If a seasoned tout declared, *'Woh picture aapko nahi chalega'*, then no further discussions were felt needed. His word was often accepted as the final one.

Procuring the tickets needed patience and perseverance and was an errand generally performed by an office peon. On occasions when the peon failed to deliver the goods, the menfolk took up the challenge themselves. On their way back home from work, they would instruct their drivers, *'Orient se lena'*. The drivers would sense the indication immediately and drive down a well tried and tested route that started at Orient and Paradise, went down Hind and Elite and if necessary, even up to Globe, Lighthouse, New Empire and Metro in the hope of at least one of those many stops proving lucky.

If none of these halls yielded any results, more plebeian options such as Gem, Jyoti, Prabhat or Grace were opted for. Venturing into the south up to Basusree and Menoka was only opted for if one came out empty handed despite combing all the lanes and by-lanes of North and Central Calcutta.

Such was the nature of their expedition, that once the goods were procured they were exhibited at home not by the name of the film but by the name of the theatre: *'Teen Jyoti matinee laya hun.'*

Sometimes, the purchase made in black was an unlucky one and the shreds of green and pink slips did not work. All dressed up, the audience would reach the theatre only to find their seats already occupied. As a consolation, the usher, who was well acquainted with such tragedies, would point his double-barrelled steel torch in the far end of the theatre, offering seats in a corner. But despite being ardent cine goers, those corners would be given a miss as they were known to be infested with bed bugs and scurrying rats and even the odd feline who needed no tickets to catwalk in.

Stalls of course were an unacceptable proposition and beneath the family's dignity. Crestfallen, the cinema outing would end sans reel.

A debacle of this sort led to bruised egos and cold receptions. 'What kind of fools do you take us to be? *Hum log ko buddhu samajhta hae?* You gave us Dress Circle tickets and this is what they turned out to be.' The tout would be served a mouthful and would generally apologise, even offering to give a second round of tickets for the same film. On him of course. But no, his equity was pronounced fallen and he was given a cold shoulder until at least the next release.

For a few years, we even had a fellow who delivered movie tickets right at our doorstep. Dressed in polyester pants with a pair of cheap sunglasses resting on his head, he stood leaning at the main gate against the iron collapsible grills that stayed pulled to one side. (The only time I remember them being full drawn and securely bolted was when the news of Indira Gandhi's assassination broke out.) Though most of us were delighted to see him and immediately congregated around him, he sparked an almost instant ire in my otherwise even tempered *Dadi* who would curse him lightly by muttering, *'Aagyo Rammaryo!'*

The *ticketwalla,* as he was called, carried a wad of precious green and pink slips—all tickets to various cine Dress Circles. He had some kind of an arrangement with several halls and for a nominal margin, would go door to door selling his spoils. Besides being resourceful, he was also a canny salesperson and knew exactly which movie could be sold to which family. Over the years, even without realising, we had revealed ourselves as a lot to him. He had observed us keenly and learnt to make offers that were too good to refuse: Bruce Lee and action film tickets to my brothers who could often be spotted with the bull worker, Shammi and later Rishi Kapoor romances to the younger *bahus* and my elder sisters, every movie that had been shot in the hills to my mother and so on. The *ticketwalla* also carried tickets to slightly more clandestine corridors of halls like Minerva, Majestic, Society and

Jamuna and knew how to peddle them delicately. He had picked up each one's Achilles heels and knew exactly where to strike!

Cinemas were also a great saviour on days that were declared a strike and cries of *'Jindabad, Jindabad'* echoed rhythmically from deserted streets. Even though many of these strikes ended by the evening, venturing out or going too far was not advisable as there was always a risk of some *gondogol* or the other. On such days we would walk across in a large group to our *parar* hall, Liberty, and consume whatever was being shown.

Women rarely stepped out entirely on their own other than going to markets and the *mandir.* They were always well escorted. There was however one occasion every year when several of them came together to form a largish all women's group and march into cinema halls to bide their time. The occasion was of *Karwa Chauth,* the day all married women held a strict fast and prayed for the well-being and longevity of their husbands. Absorbing plots unfolding on the screen helped them take their minds away from their own rumbling tummies and trim the otherwise arduous hours of the day.

For the younger lot, one of the most enjoyable bits about going to the cinemas was undoubtedly its half time: the interval. As the lights came back on, the tingling ring of an iron bottle opener brushing against glass bottles filled the air. The cold drink vendor would go from row to row, seducing customers with his multicoloured soft drinks—Campa Cola, Thums Up, Gold Spot, Limca, Bijoli's Ice-cream soda... From the other end, another vendor selling potato chips, *jhaal* chips, popcorn and patties would appear. Whenever asked, he vouched for all of his goods being absolutely *taaja.* Though the popcorn was neither fresh nor flavoured, the patties rather tepid and the chips far too oily, we would tear into these packets and secure our fistful before passing them on.

Fistfuls that were no doubt fused with stardust that has kept the matinee magic alive and kicking.

TIN
AMPAK

6

The Sack

Despite his brown skin and receding hairline, he was someone who came closest to our idea of Santa Claus. At least his sack sure did.

The loaded sack belonged to a clean shaven, benign-looking gentleman who would ritually land at our doorstep every Sunday morning, hunch down to his designated spot and greet us with a customary *'Ram Ram'*.

In less than a few seconds of him landing, the news of his arrival would spread across floors and rooms in anticipation of the loot. For his large, weather-beaten cloth sack that he lugged around was no ordinary bag. It carried a treasure trove for most of us. Remember *Chandamama* and *Champak*?

The Illustrated Weekly and *Dharmyug*? *Reader's Digest*? Or *Sportstar* with its prized tear away posters? As a child, practically nothing could match the thrill of having a new *Tintin* in hand. Or an *Asterix*. The *Commando* comics and copies of dog-eared *Archies*. *Amar Chitra Kathas*. *Pinky*. *Billoo*. *Chacha Chaudhary*. *Indrajal*. *Betal*. Oh, the list was endless.

Our dear *Kitabwala* or bookseller was our first ever mobile library who kindled the entire family with his weekly dose of magazines and lent us several comics, books and paperbacks to read at ridiculously reasonable rates. As far as I was concerned, he was one of my first introductions to the world of reading, for though our home had a lot of Indian spiritual and religious texts as well as statutory collections like the *Encyclopaedia Britannica,* those were not exactly the reads that young boys and girls were looking for.

Unknowingly, his sack became our passport to a wider world, bringing us stories that at least temporarily unshackled us from the very predictable chaotic confines of North Calcutta.

With television being restricted to Doordarshan, which was often sorry for its interruptions and cinema being limited to Hindi films, his sack was one of our easier means of being transported to a more fascinating, unknown world, away from the dreariness of the over familiar.

In a home and ecosystem, where the only languages spoken were Marwari and Hindi, he was also my gateway to English as a language rather than English as an academic subject meant for school hours only.

Though it has been more than two decades since I last saw him, his image rings fresh in my mind as if he paid us a visit only last Sunday. An extremely soft-spoken chap, perhaps in his fifties or maybe less, the only attire we ever saw him in was a colourless, cotton full-sleeved *kurta,* that may have seen better days and a *dhoti*. His ever faithful muddy-brown sack always hung from his shoulders. Within a few minutes of him settling down, he would be offered a cup of tea in a *sikora* which he would savour gratefully, emitting grunts of satisfaction.

As he sipped his tea, a raid was carried out. Each one of us knew that we needed to get our hands on the prized covers before the others did. In less than a few minutes, his very neatly arranged sack, which had fresh magazines for sale stacked on one side, Hindi novels on the other and lots of comics in between, was torn into and left disarrayed.

A copy of *Tintin* in hand or the latest *Tinkle* could arm you with great bargaining powers amongst friends and peers. Serious negotiations between cousins ensued when we could not afford to 'rent' a read individually and had to pool in our resources to rent a title for the week. Of course, the first rights of reading belonged to the one who had the largest share holding in the joint venture undertaken. Sometimes, when we couldn't afford to buy a new comic, we would quickly pull it out of his bag, while he sipped his tea and give it a read. Even if the entire comic could not be read, we managed to go through the favourite sections: *Grandma's gupshup* or *Suppandi, Humour in Uniform* or *Life's Like That*.

Kitabwala would register mild protests, saying it was new, imploring us to return it as we continued to negotiate another minute and devour it in a hurry. Never once though, do I remember him escalating the complaints to the seniors. The elders too, did not really meddle into the great fuss that carried on unless covers such as James Hadley Chase were seen changing hands.

Now calculating the damages was no ordinary affair. Spending Rs 2/- a week on some meaningless reading was taken seriously and answers had to be given to the respective mothers. *Kitabwala* had a very methodical way of keeping accounts. He carried a hard-bound *hisab khata* or an accounts diary that had green lines running through the pages and neat margins on the left hand side of every page. Right in the beginning of the year, he would dedicate a page for each one of us, with our full name and address on top. He also had our mother's name written in brackets, so he knew whom to follow up with, in case our dues began to pile up. Anyone who had two pages dedicated to his name was a very serious customer.

All his accounts would strictly be in Hindi and so we couldn't really follow what he scribbled in tiny letters against our names. Sometimes there were great debates and his book of accounts was challenged. We insisted we had not borrowed what he claimed we had, till he pulled out the rented book in question and showed us our initials on the inside back cover with a date, as proof of us having borrowed it. We would lose the case and end up settling dues in his favour. In making us do so, he didn't raise his voice, addressing us all along as so and so *bai* meaning elder sister, or so and so *babu,* though we were all at least one third his age. In fact, compared to how clearly I remember his demeanour, I have no recollection of his voice or how he sounded, except his *'Ram Ram'*, for he spoke very little. Just went about his business quietly, door to door, floor to floor.

On certain Sundays, he would come in and tell us that he would not be able to come for the next couple of weeks or so as he would be going to his village, his exact words being, *'des jayenge'*. Back then, I never quite understood what this grand destination called *des* was where everyone from the cook to the liftman, the driver and *Kitabwala* kept going away to. It just seemed to be a very faraway place where *Kitabwala* had to go to, leaving me to grapple with the deprivation of one of my single most joys of being able to lose myself between covers. It seemed rather unfair.

When we moved out of North Calcutta braving the alien world of Salt Lake, *Kitabwala* continued to visit us for a while. His manners and mode of operation remained just the same with a slight change in his look. A pair of thick black spectacles had come to sit on his benign visage and his shoulders had begun to droop a bit with the weight of the books he had been lugging around for most of his life. But his visits became more erratic as unlike the crowded homes and families of North Calcutta which kept his money bag tinkling, his visits to Salt Lake were not so viable. He had to change buses and spend a lot of time commuting in exchange for only a few magazines sold or a few books lent.

But for as long as he came his sack lit up our Sunday mornings. He helped me graduate from thin plastic-coated, alphabet books that had illustrations explaining A was for apple, to Archer, from Billoo to Blyton, Pinky to Perry Mason, Nancy Drew, Hardy Boys, Holmes, Danielle Steel, Segal, Grisham and much more. I must have spent my first decade of reading from his sack and even after two decades of him last having graced our home, if I happen to pick up a dog-eared novel or comic, the image of a well squatted, smiling *Kitabwala* sipping milky hot tea comes shining through.

7

Trring Trrring!

Other than Hindi film villains who were shown armed with a row of them in striking colours, regular households had only one such device that came in solid black and more often than not, occupied a designated spot in the drawing room.

This prized device called the telephone, comfortably served not just the entire family, but also its guests, visitors, neighbours, servants—pretty much its entire ecosystem. Families having more than one such device were the bungalow kinds with plaques like *'Niwas'* or *'House'* etched on their grand gates.

Placed on a glass-topped table, our phone would stay coyly covered with a white crocheted cloth

and was regarded as a serious device, meant for brief, purposeful communication or an exchange of important information.

Whether the exchange could take place or not, however, depended on the health and mood of the device at hand including its parentage, the telephone exchange. Though physically it was quite sturdy, its body made of heavy metal and its receiver good enough to give someone a tight whack, its constitution seemed to be somewhat fragile. As a result, on days that were marked even by the lightest showers or a hint of thunder, its wires and connection would pack up, leaving it 'dead'. In many ways, the health of the telephone was a surer weather forecast than the announcements made by the Alipore *abo-hawa daftar*.

Various kinds of cajoling would be tried to bring it out of its comatose existence. Wires would be tugged and pulled at and its vitals would be repeatedly clicked and checked so as to get even a faint murmur of a dial tone—a rather reassuring base buzz that whirred on. Sometimes the pulling and tugging worked and the dronish dial tone was heard again but more often than not, one had no such luck. The phone would be declared as dead as a doornail. Sometimes the malaise would have affected not just one individual line but an entire telephone exchange, leaving many connections in that neighbourhood, dead. Of course, it was another matter that there were men employed and dedicated to exclusively deal with telephone woes through the year. Their lives revolved around the labyrinthine corridors of the mighty Telephone Bhawan—submitting documents, filling out forms, paying bills, making applications and so on. These were men who had special powers of bringing back the dead to life.

However, on days that the phone worked, matters were different. It sat quite proudly next to the single largest book of the household—the telephone directory, a repository of an alphabetical listing along with corresponding phone numbers of all individuals, households and commercial establishments that had telephone numbers to their names. People and establishments not finding their names in the directory weren't considered to have made the cut.

Every member especially the women also tended to maintain their own personal telephone diaries. These would be small pocket-sized notebooks that lasted them several years and would fit into their personals quite effectively. Most of the numbers carefully enlisted in their own hand in these diaries would be of relations from their mother's side. The men did not bother with personal diaries. Their treasured numbers often came printed on visiting cards and they had devised an untidy but an effective way of keeping them quite handy, right next to the telephone. Every other weekend, they would simply unload the visiting cards from their briefcases and tuck the important ones under the glass panel on which sat the telephone. These cards then came to occupy the table top for months and in the process the companies they represented became a household name—Larsen & Toubro, Ellenbarrie, Jardine Henderson, Andrew Yule, BOC,

Garden Reach Shipbuilders, Tisco, Burn Standard, Indian Tobacco, Hukumchand Jute Mills and many others.

Men usually utilised the device in the mornings. Speaking in Bengali, they would generally introduce themselves by their family name on the phone. '*Newar bolchi Sir,*' was one of the first expressions I heard and picked up in Bengali. Every single person who came to the phone also had his or her own characteristic way of uttering hello. Depending on their mother tongue the 'hello' sounded either Marwari, Bihari or Bengali, the greeting's English origin having been long hijacked.

My grandmother who had never seen the sight of a classroom in her life and had come into our family when she was only twelve years old, had taught herself to memorise all the phone numbers she needed—about ten or twelve of them. She would narrate these to any one of her *bahus* in her signature style, breaking down the 5–6 digit phone number in two's so that they could dial it for her. It helped that numbers too ranged from being five to six digits only. Some of us wanted to be of help, but were quite useless until we reached a certain standard, as we didn't know numbers beyond twenty in Hindi and she couldn't narrate them in any other tongue.

The number dialling request was one that even came laced with incentives—a rare postage stamp for our collection or some such carrot. Our elders would give us a number to dial and then go back to whatever they were doing. They knew that it would be a good half an hour or more before our efforts would bear any fruit. The exercise entailed the wheel like circular dialler needing rotation six times for the number to be dialled once and the process to be repeated infinitely before a ring could be heard at the other end. More often than not, the number was always 'engaged'. The success of a ring however was celebrated joyfully, as we would holler from the drawing room to other the end of the house, *'mil gaya...'* or I've got through, to summon the concerned person to drop everything and come immediately. The holler would be even more animated and effusive if the concerned number was an out of city one, meaning if the call was an STD (Subscriber Trunk Dialling) one.

The STD calls were reserved for special people and special occasions only. An informal announcement of sorts was made before an STD number was attempted to be dialled so that all concerned members could congregate to say hello and at least hear the person's voice on the other end of the line. The usual and cheaper route of making out of station calls was through trunk dialling. One had to dial a three-digit number which was 180 and wait for an operator to answer. This operator, usually a Bengali-speaking lady, took down all the necessary details needed for booking the call, including PP or particular person, meaning she should not connect the call if that particular person was not available even if the line did go through.

A 'booking' was invariably followed by anticipation. Sometimes, the booking would come through fairly quickly but at other times, days would pass until one was forced to give up hope and re-book a call or opt for the STD route. Therefore, even a trunk call was a significant affair and though it lasted only for a few minutes, it carried with it a measure of excitement. The operator who stayed on line throughout and was privy to such conversations, promptly came to life as the call neared its three-minute duration and enquired if one wanted to end it or continue. In either case, she would always be greeted by a '*Dhonnobad Didi*' at the end of the call.

The smarter amongst us would be given the task of booking a trunk call whereas the more perseverant was assigned with dialling a local number.

The painstaking process of getting connected may have therefore been partially responsible for people raising their voices as soon as they as much as held the receiver. Throats would be cleared before embarking on an outstation call so that they could go full throttle. I think some of them even secretly believed that longer distance calls required a greater decibel for the voice to be carried the longer distance, a practice that surfaces every now and then even today on cellular technology.

Of course, no amount of raised voices could help in tackling the network getting entangled leading to a 'cross connection'. This was a commonplace scenario where a completely unknown pair of voices carried out their conversation as you endeavoured to have yours. Cross connections had a way of testing your focus—could you stay focussed on your own conversation while strangers spoke alongside? The choice in such a scenario was a Hobson's one. One could either choose to ignore the strange voices and continue with the call or hang up, which came with the risk of not getting through again. Sometimes, I heard our seniors reach out to the other voices, requesting them to leave the line; imploring them that theirs was the more serious of the two calls. *'Dada, apni rekhe din na... aamar call ta khoob dorkari!'* If lucky, such requests would get honoured and the line would clear up. At other times, there would be an argument over who had dialled and got through first and the more resilient caller would end up continuing with his call.

The phone was a device used almost exclusively by elders. Children getting a phone call was an absolutely rarity. If we had to make a phone call, a full enquiry was conducted first—who was the call to, what was it for and finally what were the contents of the conversation. However, our roles assumed some importance each time there was a call for a neighbour or guest, where we had to run, find the concerned person in a jiffy and ensure that he came to the line. It was perfectly acceptable that our phone number was given out by our neighbours and theirs by us. In fact, the main door which was left ajar through the day saw all kinds of people walking in and out just to receive phone calls. It was all well understood and accommodated.

What were frowned upon were idle conversations or a purposeless call. None of the elders could fathom the need to talk to a friend who we had just spent half a day with at school or college and would be meeting only the next day again.

What could possibly be so important that could not wait for the next day? Chatting on the phone was reckoned to be a bad habit and a waste of time. Many of us therefore, warmly greeted the mushrooming PCOs where one could feed a coin and make a non-prying call.

One of the highlights of visiting the family's official and commercial quarters in Dalhousie was seeing the number of telephones in action. There were at least two and sometimes even three such devices on every table. The tables having multiple telephones were usually occupied by the senior males of the clan. The operator, a mild mannered *bhodrolok* who sat for years dialling and transferring calls seemed to be by far the busiest and most important officer of the establishment. Office after office on every floor resonated with the un-orchestrated chorus created by typewriters, rotary phones and telephone rings as pendulum clocks marked the hours till 5 pm every working day.

The business of procuring a new phone line was nothing short of a test of one's character.

Parchment upon parchment had to be inked, palms had to be gently greased and many queues suffered before there could even be a ray of hope. After months of waiting however, when a new connection and a brand new phone box did enter the household, it would almost be like welcoming a baby into the family. *Bakshish* would be doled out generously sometimes accompanied by sweets and at least a few members would break into a joyous celebration.

It was on one such occasion when the wait had been particularly laborious and the case had dragged on unendingly, that our collective sense of euphoria on getting a telephone connection was so profound that my brother broke into poetry, penning a poem for the occasion!

He had appropriately titled his verse *'Trrring Trrring!'*

EELER
KALKA MAIL
END-2
X

8

Chhuk-Chhuk Gaadi

Remember Ashok Kumar's *'Railgaadi chhuk chhuk chhuk chhuk...'* from *Ashirwad*? Or Kavi Pradeep's *'Aao bachchon tumhe dikhayein...'* from *Jagriti*? *Apu* and *Durga* chasing the train in *Pather Panchali* or Uttam-Sharmila in *Nayak*? Or Jatayu's maiden appearance when he befriends Feluda in a train? Alright, let's move away from the black-and-white era and inch closer to today's Indian cinema—*Sholay, DDLJ, Jab We Met*....

Can any of these stories be complete without their iconic train scenes and the role played by the railways?

Actually, the Indian Railways has always been somewhat of an over the top, chaotic and dramatic deal, yet has commanded an endearing appeal

for generations. Coming from a generation when airplanes were limited to the ones that were crafted out of paper, tossed in the air for a moment and quickly forgotten, it was the train journeys and all the drama that came with them that occupied the bulk of our travel diaries.

To begin with, many starting from the *coolies,* to the drivers including several members of the family, did not refer to them as trains, opting instead for the more colloquial term *gaadi.* They had probably picked up the term from the frequent announcements that reverberated across platforms in Hindi and it had got etched into their vocabularies. Platforms were however, called platforms—so the duo was referred to as such and such *gaadi* coming on platform number so and so.

You didn't have to be a traveller yourself to be touched by the tumult of trains. Since we were not very far from the Howrah station, every other day somebody from the family was assigned with either picking up or dropping off someone to the station. Along with the deputed adult, a younger member would often get thrown in as a lackey. The idea of a brisk adieu by a simple wave of hand and a wish for safe travels was inconceivable.

The key challenge in collecting someone was getting there on time. The infamous traffic jams of Howrah often lived up to their reputation and there were many instances when we got out of the car and walked the last furlong to Howrah to make it in the nick of time. Traffic jams were estimated depending on the time of the day and the day of the week. There were days when lorries from *Machhua Bazaar* or rituals near Satyanarayan Park were bound to throw traffic off gear. At other times, the reception party would be in place but the train would be running late, demanding a test of patience—in such cases, we killed time, loitering around at the platform since returning home and making a second trip to the station was not an option either.

Seeing someone off came with elaborate rituals. It started with the *roli-chawal teeka* applied on the forehead to ward off evil, a sweet something be it a *laddoo, sandesh* or just a piece of *misri* given for a sweet journey ahead and the handing over of an envelope which contained a princely sum of eleven or sometimes twenty-one rupees as an auspicious token. Each traveller would then duly touch the feet of all elders present and take leave.

The assigned family member who was responsible for the see-off would then get into action. His job was to ensure that the traveller/s made it safely to the station, found his allocated seat and felt duly settled with his luggage and other belongings securely tucked in. It was only once the conductor waved his green flag and blew his whistle, would the two parties finally bid adieu to each other; the adieu often unashamedly tearful at both ends. One of the most poignant goodbyes that I witnessed from the corner of my eye every summer was of my mother weeping like a child each time we left the hills behind and headed to the New Jalpaiguri Station to catch our train to Kolkata. As soon as we reached the Teesta river, she would fling a fistful of coins through the car window into it and bow in tearful reverence.

Whether one was settled in life or not, feeling settled in trains was an absolute must. Since train journeys were often long and schedules notoriously erratic, every passenger carried his pet belongings and necessary supplies so as to feel at home.

Since we travelled in sizeable groups, we came with multiple curious accoutrements and paraphernalia: suitcases and trunks, beddings, vanity cases, odd bags, tiffin boxes and the very important *pani ka jharna* or a water carrier with an inbuilt washable glass. Travelling light wasn't an idea we were familiar with. Luckily the Ambassador further fortified with a steel carrier installed on its roof, was good enough to carry our world as well as the many of us in it.

As soon as we reached our designated platform and alighted from the car, the long march to the two-tier AC berth would begin. Howrah always had coolies—the men who in their flaming red robes, faded *dhotis* and brass badges knew exactly which family needed their burdens to be carried and would promptly come to our rescue. Even before anybody could utter a full sentence, they would quickly form a group of two or three and start lifting our luggage, stacking the suitcases on their cloth-lined heads, flinging the bags on to their arms. With cries of *'siiidee....siiiddeee...'* the coolies then raced through the platform perhaps in order to end their misery as quickly as possible and deposited us precisely at our seats. After some heated negotiations over their fees, they would leave and we would get down to adjusting every piece of our freshly stencilled luggage, courtesy Shankar Agency, New Market, securing each piece with a chain and a padlock.

Of the entire luggage, the trickiest was by far the bedding—a stubbornly un-negotiable rotund piece of roll that was unfolded and piled onto a berth to provide for some padding and thereby a comfortable snooze at night. Of course, despite all the preparation for a comfortable night's sleep, each bogey had at least one irrepressible snorer who would keep half the bogey awake or cursing. Pre-equipped with a feather pillow and a blanket, the beddings went out of fashion once the Railways started providing bed sheets, pillows and blankets.

Starting a train journey without stopping at a ubiquitous A H Wheeler stall was out of question. Pooling in our resources including dipping into the freshly received envelopes, we would pick out magazines, comics and 'story books'. Fewer joys came close to the joy of being snugly tucked in an upper berth, reading against a night light or listening to a story being read out as the train gently rocked you to sleep. With the curtains drawn and the lights other than the reading or night lights out, the compartment would become quite cosy and slumber set in effortlessly.

Dawn always broke earlier than usual and mornings in trains remained its busiest hour. Queues were formed for the basin as well as the bathroom after reliable reports came in as to which of the two bathrooms located at the two ends was less of a mess. I don't know why in all the packing, we didn't think of packing in more than one tube of toothpaste or toilet paper roll because invariably there would be a scramble for both. Vendors and *feriwalas* of all kinds went from coach to coach calling out their wares—'*cha cha, lebu cha, 'tesman, jhal muri bolun jhal muri, Nescafe'* and so on… If the train came equipped with a pantry car, the attendant would soon come in with options of breakfast—toast, omelette, sandwich, *cha.* But a Marwari family that opted for a pantry car breakfast or meal wasn't quite worth its salt.

In fact, one of the most enjoyable episodes in any train journey was its food—simple but wholesome homemade *puris* fried in *kadhais,* two dry *sabzis,* one of which had to be an *aalu* preparation, at least two types of *achaar,* again one of which had to be *mirchi,* finely crushed *papad* to which were added salt, red chilli powder and a few drops of ghee and some sort of a *meetha—laddoos* or *sandesh.* Plastic was not in vogue and the food was neatly packed in cardboard boxes. The plates used to eat were simple leaf platters or *pattals,* made out of dried leaves and stitched together with toothpicks. Meals were had quite timely and in an organised way. Old newspapers, brought specifically for meals were first laid out on the lower berths as each person held his plate out for the goodies to be served. Second helpings were common. Actually, there was something quite inexplicable about how appetites got worked up in trains—was it the group travel or the excitement of the journey? Did the regular home-cooked food acquire some special ambrosial quality via the railway perambulation? Of course, there was always enough to offer to co-passengers and in the process make friends with them. Sometimes, great friendships were struck and numbers and addresses exchanged. It was most natural to introduce your entire family travelling and explain the purpose and route of your travel in detail. '*Bachchon ki chhuttiyan hae na... Dilli tak jayenge. Phir Kathgodam se Nainital. Aur aap log?*'

The meals that were so painstakingly prepared, packed and laid out elaborately were gobbled up in no time. One or two of us were then assigned to clear it all up and we would hop over to the bin near the vestibule to chuck the waste. It was at this point where men chose to congregate—leaning against the open gate, soaking in the fresh breeze and sometimes stealing a puff or two. Fields and towns whizzed past and the speeding train created the illusion of moving tracks. Sometimes a speeding train from the opposite direction would cross ours, both trains letting out whistles to alert each other. At such a juncture, arithmetic problems would be discussed and explained: 'If train A is moving at such and such speed covering a distance of x km, then at what point will it cross Train B which is moving in the opposite direction at so and so speed....'

Trains lent themselves to games and fairly cerebral ones at that. Since movement was restricted and one had a lot of time at hand, cards, Ludo, chess and other board games were packed to add colour to the journey. Other games like memory or dumb charades were even easier to break into since they did not require any props and could be played without any fuss. Co-passengers and neighbours freely joined in. But when travelling in a group, nothing came close to the charm of *antakshari* which easily lasted for an hour or two and where everybody participated in merry gusto, whether they could hold a note or not. Interestingly, even with the vocal chords and zeal remaining competitive for long, very rarely did a clear winner ever emerge after a round of *antakshari.*

Sometimes, our games were interrupted by the arrival of the Ticket Collector or TC, the man who was clearly identifiable by his white shirt, black coat and tie. He carried with him a sheet of paper which had the names of all the passengers travelling. A similar sheet could be found pasted with *leyi* on each coach near the gate and one of us would ensure that we had tallied our seat numbers before climbing in. There were times when we were perfectly at ease with the TC's arrival as we would all be sitting as per our assigned numbers with confirmed tickets in hand. But it wasn't always so smooth sailing. Sometimes, we were short by one or two seats which had remained in the 'waiting list' but we had boarded the train nonetheless. The accepted norm was to share the berth, show the wait-list ticket along with the bunch of confirmed seats and 'settle' the matter with the TC. At other times, despite all seats being confirmed, they would not be allocated together splitting the group across bogeys and coaches. Sometimes, the TC could manage to resolve the situation by reshuffling the seats but at other times we were left with no choice but to be seated apart. For years, well after crossing the prescribed age limit, several of us continued to be booked in 'half ticket' as it cost fifty percent less. We even got away each time!

Sometimes we would drift away from our usual two-tier AC to travel by first-class AC Coupe, an occurrence that happened only if we'd failed to get reservation in our usual order. The first-tier AC that came with cleaner linen and an in-built washbasin, felt like one's very own tiny citadel once the compartment was locked. Tiny roaches however, not needing any tickets, crept in there too.

Journeying into the hill stations of Mussoorie, Nainital or Himachal meant two train rides—one till Ajmeri Gate or Paharganj, New Delhi and one thereafter. The second leg was often the shorter one and was accomplished in a narrow-gauge train in the First Class. The train window would throw up visuals that changed every second. Dust and heat notwithstanding this was the most fun train journey of all. We would read the names of all the many stations we passed by and get an up close view of the flurry of activity that went on at each when the train halted. Vendors came right up to the windows selling all kinds of things—a non-stop call for tea, coffee, water, freshly cut fruits and vegetables, pickled berries, *chaat* and whatnot. At bigger junctions it was thrilling to step out onto the pavement for just a few minutes and come face-to-face with your family from the other side.

Despite them being unfailingly chaotic, very often erratic and inconvenient in so many ways, there continues to be a remarkable charm about train journeys; a charm that equips you with a vital lesson for life—that it is as important to enjoy the journey as it may be to arrive.

9

Homemade

A pitched battle continued between us and the crows. The scavengers would gather in large numbers, cawing loudly as they eyed the goods. Even if our attempts to shoo them fell short and one or two of them got lucky, my *Dadi* never failed to scare them away. Though diminutive in size, the resolute *belan* in her hand and the reprimand on her tongue were enough to keep the crows at bay.

After all, the *papads* laid out to dry on the *chhath* were the result of a great deal of skill and toil and were not to be taken lightly. Though my mum, all my aunts and some of my sisters did play a role in the annual operation of *papads* being made at home, the boys were spared entirely (*ladkon ka kaam thodi hae!)* and were entrusted only with guarding them. Since I was still too young to be participating in the making of it, I joined the boys in playing guard at the terrace where hundreds of *papads* were laid out on bamboo *chattais* under the winter sun for them to dry before they could be stored in large steel canisters for the year.

The *papad*-making operation was not an ordinary one. All the womenfolk pooled in their time, skill and talent as they rolled out hundreds of balls of finely ground pulses, mixed with all kinds of spices and oil, into perfect circular, wafer thin sheets. While they were collectively at it, somewhat of a friendly competition ensued—if one could prepare a delectable dough, the other could roll it out paper thin; if one was fast, the other was meticulous. The exercise that carried on for a good week left the entire house smelling of freshly prepared *papad*. Much of it was also sent out to relatives and neighbours who looked forward to receiving their annual quota of this homemade crunchy treat.

With vegetable markets being fresh and bountiful, winters were also a great time to prepare all kinds of *achaars.* Tender radishes, carrots, potatoes, green chilli peppers and lemon were carefully selected for the purpose. The vegetables were purchased in large quantities and had to be evenly sliced and chopped before they could be finely marinated in a carefully prepared concoction of aromatic spices and oils. If preparing *papads* required labour, preparing *achaars* needed a sense of sharp olfactory, perfect proportions and a seasoned, masterful hand. Not a single winter went by when the verandas were not dotted with at least two or three glass jars, packed to their lids with *achaars,* their mouths covered with muslin, left to marinate richly in the sun. Despite so many elders keeping a hawk eye, we never failed to secretly unlid them and enjoy a lick or two.

If *achaars* could help you get through the dullest meal and were the perfect accompaniment for hot *parathas,* freshly churned white butter made the combination ethereally complete and sinful. Every morning, at a fixed time and a reserved spot in the kitchen, *Dadi* could be seen rhythmically tugging the strings of her *bilona,* churning fresh butter and ghee out of milk. A couple of us squatted around her, taking in her delicious banter, greedily awaiting our first dollops of the goodies. The clarified butter would then be used for cooking and some of it reserved for lighting *diyas* in the *mandir*.

Afternoons were remarkably different from mornings that were full of hustle and bustle. With the menfolk busy at work, the children either at school or play and the domestic helpers resting in their quarters, afternoons were undisturbed and much quieter. After rejuvenating themselves with a well-earned siesta, the women resorted to their respective sewing kits, knitting needles and embroidery baskets to spend the next couple of hours until the rush of the evening kicked in.

On days more mundane, they would do minor mending only—a stitch here, a monogram or an alteration there. Since all of them only wore sarees, there would invariably be a new one that needed 'fall and pico'—final touches that were given to a new saree to smoothen out its frayed edges and readied so that it would pleat and fall well. The Singer and later the Usha sewing machines helped them achieve this task in a matter of just a few minutes. Our contribution in it all was to spring the machine into action by rotating its handle and continuing to do so till the stitches needed to be rolled out—a role that we could not play when the machines were upgraded and the handle was replaced by the foot pedal.

On other days they would pull out their elaborate needle work in progress and resume from where they'd left it. Bedcovers, cushion covers, table cloths and napkins on which were traced out intricate patterns and designs to be filled up with multicoloured embroidery using all sorts of difficult stitches and delicate French knots. I was fascinated by the names of the stitches though I could learn to do very few of them: running, back, blanket, buttonhole, herringbone, chain, etc. My aunts, on the other hand, couldn't really care about these

English names—they'd given each one their own description and nick name and that's what the stitches went by.

Sometimes their designs were self-conceived; at other times, inspired by magazines and even items for sale at shops such as Good Companions. Foreign cross-stitch books that often had their notations in Chinese were a rage and a great favourite of my mother's. Fastidious as she was, she took great pains to lay out matching threads, an assortment of needles and other bits and bobs. Proceeding to understand the detailed pattern, she'd then go hole by hole as she patiently threaded in the counter stitches to produce cross-stitched masterpieces, many of which became family heirloom.

The craft that I enjoyed watching the most however, was knitting. Come winter and bright hued, soft woollen balls often purchased from Lepcha Bazaars in the hills, would come out of their storages along with silver-grey, long, pointed needles. Such was their mastery over knitting that they never needed to consult a design on paper—

the entire design was composed in their heads as they went along, almost like how an Indian classical maestro improvises during a recital. They could knit at such a pace that often the needles could not be seen; only a steady, periodic clicking of the needles could be heard. So, while our needle work classes at school taught us knitting in a bookish way—knit one, pearl two—these women who had never attended a needle work class, had learnt and mastered it organically. It was fascinating to watch the lifeless, rolled-up wool acquire shape, form and life with every newly knitted row. Each of them managed to conjure scarves, mufflers, vests and sweaters every winter—all to be gifted or worn by other members of the family. Rarely did I see any of the women make something for themselves.

The homemade activities also offered room for challenges and bets. Could anyone dare to carve out the icing on a cake, the way Kathleen's did? But those wagering these bets did not know the strength of innovative, household hacks. What was a one line icing of whipped cream on a cake, for women who had watched intricate *mehendi* being applied on hands for years? Deftly, they prepared new plastic cones, filled them up with homemade cream and a firm hand did the rest. They could match any baker's icing even without using proper nozzles.

Much of this handcrafted affair was a Venus-driven domain. The men though, could hardly be blamed as they were squarely in charge of the factories and therefore, of the factory made.

Their do-it-yourself skills at home were much humbler: neatly folded airplanes, tightly wound spinning tops, well-tied kites and the like. But their ability to flawlessly add, subtract and juggle rows of numbers in their heads, repair fuses or render a perfect engineering drawing on paper never failed to impress us.

Whether we were inspired by all this or whether it was plainly due to the fact that spending money on gifts was not encouraged, many of us learnt to nurture some creativity by crafting imperfect homemade gifts. Poems were scribbled on handy rough paper—discarded bills and office documents, old exercise books or brown paper and later 'faired' out on a good blank card in neat handwriting. Still life was sketched on canvas or on paper and later filled in with colour. These would then be turned into greeting cards or wall art. Posters of all sizes featuring sportsmen or other famous personalities would be made with poster paint and then pasted on obscure corners. Girls eligible for marriage, already taking special classes aimed at giving their bio-data an advantage, lit up table tops with their flower arrangement or Bonsai. Some others, who had learnt to carve vegetables, produced decorative salads for meals. For particularly significant occasions such as milestone birthdays or weddings, some of us would spend days to compose an appropriate parody or song and practise it until we could render it well. Those who could not sing but enjoyed music went to great lengths to get customised cassettes that would have been hard to find, favourite tracks sourced and recorded one after the other. These tapes would then be given fancy titles such as 'From me to you' or 'Golden Collection'.

Despite the best of global brands now easily available and within the reach of many, the handmade is making a huge comeback in every corner of the world. In many cases it is also far more expensive and goes by more flattering terms such as sustainable, eco-friendly, limited edition and more.

Receiving something handmade truly makes a very special statement—a statement that someone cared enough to put in his time, effort and expression in order to convey a thought. And, as we do know but perhaps need to be reminded of every now and then, it is the thought that counts the most.

10

To Market, To Market...

It was an age when a purchase of any sort was permissible and made only when deemed necessary—during special occasions, weddings and so on. Whimsical purchases were rare and even those came with some doses of admonishment or guilt. Kitchen supplies came in bulk and were stored in large boxes and containers in a cool, dark ante chamber called the *bhandaar* near the kitchen.

Many suppliers regularly came home to sell their wares: from the *bakarkhaniwala* who carried a variety of breads in his large tin box to the *bartanwali* who sold all kinds of pots and pans and retrieved used tin cans, her sharp nasal call matching the clanging of her wares.

There were fancier vendors too: a fair and handsome Kashmiri *shawlwala* who came with the onset of winters, a *sareewala* who visited throughout the year, an *attarwala* who carried a small box filled with tiny glass bottles and cotton swabs and a Jain jeweller who showed up with a black briefcase which he took great pains in locking on his way out.

The vendors were completely at ease in opening up their parcels and heaps, setting up shop and displaying their wares with panache at home. With his nimble fingers, the *shawlwala* pulled his *pashminas* through a ring, vouching for their authenticity and the *sareewala* used the broad shoulders of his young helper to drape the yards and show off the *palla*. The jeweller on the other hand chose to operate alone, perhaps because his goods were far more delicate—pearls and semi-precious stones. He'd keep them carefully wrapped in layers of cotton laced with tracing paper, tucked in metallic pencil boxes, each one carefully labelled.

The women on their part got together in twos and threes, admiring the goods, double checking for quality and sometimes pulling out their personal savings stored in envelopes and small pouches to even make a purchase. Over the years, they had acquired an eye for quality workmanship and goods and had also sharpened their bargaining skills. The vendors on their part had come to understand the tastes and preferences of their customers as well as sized up their pockets. The shop at home arrangement was doorstep delivered retail therapy that worked well for many years.

Not that we looked at it as shopping, but one of our earliest escapades into a market of any sort were our frequent visits to the mile-long College Street. Somebody or the other would drop us off at Bow Bazar *mor* and the remaining distance would be covered on foot or by a short tram ride. Lined by luminous academic institutions, the eponymous College Street and its *boi para* held us in absolute fascination. Countless shops sat cheek by jowl next to one another with books spilling onto the pavement, run by their respective proprietors who knew every title they possessed. The proprietors also had an uncanny knack of figuring out exactly what you were looking for in less than a glance—medical or engineering; secondary or higher secondary, fiction or reference. Though the purchases were nominal the browsing was indefinite and long. College Street was a market that had served several generations sans MRP. It was therefore, also one of the first places where we witnessed bargains and negotiations made for every purchase. We also saw how shopkeepers took pride in their wares and did not fail to tick off a customer who tried to bargain too hard. *'Eta macher bajaar na! Onno jayega dekhun.'*

If there were still any items that needed to be purchased, there was always the neighbourhood *Ram Mandir* or the vast *Burrabazar.* And of course, New Market. The market that went by the adage, *'Ekhane ki na pawa jaye? Baagher doodh o pawa jaye!'*

But nobody in the family or even the extended clan knew New Market like *Maa* did. My earliest memories of it are rushing through its labyrinth corridors, tailing my mother as she navigated its messy, odorous grid in a hurry. Every time she'd got the family car to run an errand or visit a relative, she'd make a quick detour and pop into New Market.

I'm not sure that she purchased very much. Neither was her pocket spilling over nor would any kind of excess be appreciated at home. But New Market for her wasn't ever about a big purchase. She had befriended the diversity it offered albeit via ungainly passages and negotiating those unaided had given her the confidence to be joyfully lost.

It allowed her to forge goodwill with unfamiliar shopkeepers who would welcome her into their shops, referring to her as *didi* or *memsahib,* a departure from the usual reference of *binni ji* or *bahu ji.* She in turn, also knew each one by his first name and added a *bhaiya* to it when referring to them. Through their painstaking salesmanship she would traverse the world of French laces and

Swiss watches; of English bone china tea sets and Spanish porcelain. Scurrying through its corridors, she would pick up items that were considered to be quite exotic for the family kitchen: Ajinomoto, Bandel cheese, vinegar, soya sauce, vanilla essence; wooden spoons and tin cans for baking cakes and dishes and so on.

An annual brush with New Market, for some of us was when we would get promoted to the next class and would get new, shiny, wooden school boxes with our names painted on them. Hardly anybody carried backpacks then and *Maa* would happily take us to her pet shop, Shankar Agency, where they would greet her warmly, offer us a seat fashioned out of an iron trunk along with a *thanda* (one bottle to be shared by two people) while they'd carefully stencil our names in white on our chosen boxes.

On days when she had a little more leisure time at hand, *Maa* would indulge in the unimaginable. She would go to the rear end of the market and after a quick glance both ways, slip into Karcos for an egg roll. Coming from a household where even onions and garlic could not be cooked, this was nothing short of sacrilege. But ironically, it was the crowd and confusion of New Market that shielded her from any glare.

Even if nobody had accompanied her to New Market, there were telltale signs of her having visited it. On such days a corner of her room would be lit up by long-stemmed colourful gladiolas only available there. I suspect that she went there both for the flowers as well as for the chance to converse in Nepali, for a few of the florists were from the hills and warmly referred to her as *boini.* In transacting with them, she was transported even if briefly to the hills.

For a place that's called 'New', New Market is both old and unkempt. Over the years, its mess has only grown manifold. Hawkers eat up its pavements, making the vehicles blare incessantly for space. Its lanes continue to be littered and often waterlogged in the monsoons. Its material decay is no doubt a pitiful sight. Yet if one looks closely enough, many of the shopkeepers and customers appear to be joyously involved in whatever they are doing.

In an age of instant gratification, New Market stands tall like an old flame of Calcutta; its clock tower lying unwound, telling the time exactly as it stands there and in many other nooks and crannies of the city: still.

Glossary

Aagyo Rammaryo: *Aagyo*—to arrive; *rammaryo*—is a Marwari curse used to point out someone evil. However, it was used in a jocular way for someone who was a nuisance or disliked

Aarti: A ritual in which lights soaked in ghee are lit and offered to the divine

Abo-hawa daftar: The meteorological office

Achaar: Pickle

Adda: A free-wheeling, spontaneous chat session where people freely participate in, and a range of topics are discussed.

Aalu: Potato

Antakshari: A popular game where two teams compete with each other, singing songs. The first team begins with a song and the second one picks up a new song that starts with the letter on which the previous song has ended

Aur khoobusrati se long on ke aage se jaati hui, gend boundary line par: The ball has been hit smoothly to cross 'long on' and is heading towards the boundary line

Ayah didi: Female helper, often like a nanny who would be addressed as *didi* or sister

Babu: A title used for an educated man; also denotes seniority and status

Bachchon ki chhutiyan hae na... Dilli tak jayenge. Phir Kathgodam se Nainital. Aur aap log?: The children have their summer holidays. So we're going to Nainital via Delhi and Kathgodam. How about you all?

Bai: Elder sister; also used as a suffix in a woman's name to denote respect

Bakarkhaniwala: Bread vendor who carries an assortments of freshly baked breads

Baksheesh: A token monetary tip of a small amount rendered for services offered. The baksheesh is often followed by a *salaam*—an acknowledgement from the recipient

Bandh: A form of protest similar to a general strike during which shops and other commercial establishments are closed and public transport is affected. Bengal has been infamous for its *bandhs*

Bandhgala: Originating in Jodhpur, a *Bandhgala* is a suit worn by men for formal occasions and parties

Bartanwali: A woman who sells utensils, often cheap ones

Belan: Rolling pin

Bhadrolok: A term typically used to describe Bengalis who are considered to be well educated and somewhat prosperous

Bhaiya: Elder brother

Bhandaar: Store

Bilona: Manual process of churning milk into butter

Binni ji/Bahu ji: The correct term was Beenani—a Marwari word meaning bride. Its pronunciation however got reduced to Binni ji or daughter-in-law

Boi para: Literally meaning a neighbourhood of books

Boini: Sister in Nepali

Bow Bazar mor: The crossing of Bow Bazar

Cha, Cha: Tea, tea!

Chaat: Popular street food in India vended out of carts and stalls. Serves as a snack

Chattais: Light weight, easy to roll up floor mats

Chaupad: Also called *Chausar*. A board game where the board is made of cloth, pawns of wood and dice of cowry

Chhath: Terrace

Choolah: An earthen or a brick stove used for cooking

Chota: Small

Chowk: A open-air courtyard in the centre of a building. The chowk becomes visible from most corners of the building and is often the place that buzzes with social activity

Chudi: Fine rings of cloth that gather around the ankle, one on top of another, making it look like a set of bangles

Churidar: Tightly fitting trousers that get narrower, revealing the contours of the leg. Worn by men and women

Commi/Capi: Slang for a communist or a capitalist

Dada, apni rekhe din na… amar call ta khoob dorkari!: Brother, please hang up… my call is really important!

Dadi: Paternal grandmother

Des jayenge: Leaving for one's hometown

Dhonnobad Didi: Thank you, sister

Dhoti: Crafted out of a long rectangular piece of cloth which is wrapped around the legs and knotted at the waist, a dhoti is the traditional menswear of Rajasthan as well as Bengal. For everyday purposes, cotton dhotis are worn whereas silk maybe chosen for special occasions

Dhuniya: Cotton carder

Diya: A small oil lamp made out of baked clay which is lit with a wick

Ek ka teen: One for the price of three. Slang used to quote a high price and then bargain

Ekhane ki na pawa jaye? Baagher doodh o pawa jaye!: What can you not get here? Even tiger's milk can be found!

Eta macher bajaar na! Onno jayega dekhun: This is not a fish market. Check elsewhere

Fall and pico: A standard finishing touch given to a saree after it is purchased. A rectangular piece of cloth is stitched at the bottom from the inside to its edges, to provide it a good fall. Hence the name, fall. A pico is done to close any frayed or loose edges

Feriwala: Pedlars and roundsmen who roam around villages and cities selling all kinds of wares

Gaddi: Originally denoted a place or an address from where commercial activity was carried out. Marwari business families therefore operated out of a *gaddi*. The word came to be used in a residential context too, to denote the main room where the family gathered. Equivalent of a drawing room

Gaadi: Car

Gondogol: When you sense a problem or chances of trouble

Gupshup: Chit chat

Hanuman Chalisas: A devotional hymn comprising forty verses recited for Lord Hanuman. Chanting or reciting these verses, penned by poet Goswami Tulsidas is supposed to invoke Hanuman's divine intervention and protect one in times of danger

Hartal: Similar to a bandh

Hisab Khata: A book of accounts

Hum log ko buddhu samajhta hae?: Do you take us to be fools?

Iskool: School pronounced with an Indian accent

Iskool mein kya hua? Parikcha tha kya?: What happened at school today? Was there an exam?

Janeu: A sacred thread worn over the left shoulder; predominant amongst Brahmins

Jhaal: Spicy

Jhal muri: A spicy concoction of puffed rice

Jhol: Gravy in a curry

Jindabad, Jindabad: An expression used to offer encouragement to a movement or an idea. The correct pronunciation though is *zindabad* but in Bengal, the 'z' becomes a 'j'

Kadhai: A deep cooking wok often made of steel or brass

Karwa Chauth: A day of fasting by women for their husbands so that they may be blessed with a long and safe life

Khali-khali: A chant used by bus conductors to convey that seats are available. *Khali* literally means empty

Khul ja sim sim: A mantra from the popular Arabic story, *Ali Baba and 40 Thieves* in which it is the code used to open locked caves full of jewels and valuables. It has come to mean a magic mantra that unlocks prosperity

Kirtan: Devotional chants set to music sung by a group of singers, with one of them being the lead singer

Kitabwala: Vendor of books

Kon class?: Which class?

Kurta-pajama: A loosely fitted tunic that ends near the knees is called a kurta whereas its bottom half is called a pajama. The style and fabric change according to occasion

Laddoo: An Indian sweet made by rolling a mixture of flour, sugar, ghee and other ingredients into a ball. Laddoos of all kinds are made in Indian homes and also offered to the Gods

Ladkon ka kaam thodi hae: Boys shouldn't have to do this job

Lakshman Rekha: The episode features in the Indian epic *Ramayana* when Lakshman, the younger brother of Lord Ram draws a circle within which Sita must confine herself if she is to avoid any trouble. The circle came to be eponymously called Lakshman Rekha. Figuratively, it is used to denote a protective boundary set by someone

Lebu cha: Lemon tea

Leyi: Glue

Light aa gaya: The electricity is back

Maharaj: The head cook in a large family. Instead of being addressed by his name, he is called Maharaj or even Maharaj *ji*

Manjira: A traditional percussion instrument used to keep beat in Indian folk music. Made out of a pair of small hand cymbals

Meetha: Sweet

Meetha-saada: A betel leaf wrapped with condiments to give it a slightly sweet flavour

Memsahib: A colonial term used to address modern or upwardly women in India

Mil gaya: I've got it

Mirchi: Chilli

Misri: Large sugar crystals

Mitti ka tel: Kerosene oil

Mor: A crossing

Niwas: Family house often handsome or opulent

Orient se lena: Take the route that starts from Orient

Padya Bharti: A textbook of Hindi poetry

Palla: The loose, undraped end of a saree; also often its most attractive part

Pallu: The loose, unpleated end of a saree, often used to cover the head

Pandal: A temporary structure built for religious festivals. Very common during Durga Puja in Bengal when innumerable pandals are constructed thus giving birth to the term 'pandal hopping'

Pani ka jharna: A water carrier that may hold several glasses of water at once

Papad: Thin, crisp and disc-shaped, a papad is made out of a mixed dough and can either be roasted or fried

Parar: Of the neighbourhood

Paras: Neighbourhoods

Paratha: Literally meaning layers of cooked dough, a paratha is a popular flat bread made out of baking whole wheat dough on a skillet

Pashmina: An expensive shawl made out of goat's wool

Patloon: Pants or trousers

Pattal: Plates made out of large, dried leaves

Permit Raj: Also called the License Raj. A term used to denote an era of red tapism

Puri: Small, round and deep fried, a puri is made of wheat flour and served with curry

Ram naam satya hae: A chant that is heard when a dead body is being carried on the shoulders for cremation. It is also a way of explaining that you carry nothing with you on your final journey, except the Lord's name

Ram Ram: An ancient Hindu way of greeting someone. May have been started when Valmiki who by chanting Ram Ram was transformed from an evil dacoit to a great sage

Roli-chawal teeka: An auspicious application of roli and rice applied on the forehead, between the eyebrows. The particular point is supposed to be a spiritual one having the power to help us connect with our inward self. Roli is also called kumkum and is made out of turmeric and lime stone

Rona dhona: Wailing and weeping

Sabzis: Curries

Safas: A manually tied, traditional headdress worn by men. The colour and style of tying a safa indicates the person's social class and caste. On occasions such as marriages, all the menfolk of the family have ornate safas, bedecked with jewels tied to their heads

Sandesh: Bengali sweets made out of milk, sugar, cottage cheese and other ingredients

Seth: A title used for a person belonging to a high social status. Could also be a merchant

Shawlwala: A shawl salesman

Sherwani: A long coat-like garment worn over a kurta by men for a formal look. Often teamed with a pair of churidars. Also called *achkan*

Siiide Siiide: An informal call made aloud by someone on the move, asking for people to step aside

Sikora: Traditional handle-less clay cup used to drink tea

Sil katao: Sil is a flat stone used for grinding spice mixes in Indian cuisine using a batta, a cylindrical grinding stone. 'Sil katao' means etching the grinding stones to sharpen them

Surma: Kohl or *kaajal,* an eyeliner that is applied on the eyelids. Generally applied by women more than men

Taaja: Fresh. The correct pronunciation though is 'taaza'

'tesman: Colloquial pronunciation of a noted English daily, *The Statesman*

Thakar ji: Men who were of a certain age were not addressed by their name out of respect. Instead, a generic name was coined for them and that is what they went by. Thakar was a Marwari way of addressing someone who hailed from the Thakur community. A 'ji' was added for respect. The adage remained so consistent with the name that it almost became an extension of it

Thanda: Cold

Ticketwala: Vendor of tickets

Kaleidoscope

Aamar Kolkata

Khawa-daawa, adda-golpo, Robindra Sangeet,
Sarobar-e jog-byaam-e thaki phit.

Boyi kinte hole jaayi College Street,
Nondon-e film festival always heet!

Maa Kalir pujo dite jaayi amra Kalighat,
Kena kaata korte hole nothing but Goriahat!

Mera Kalkatta

Din ki shuruaat hoti hae Victoria ke round kaat kar,
Rakhte hain share bajaar ke utaar-chadhav par kadi najar.

Chalaate hain dukaane, karkhaane aur karobaar,
Khariddaari matlab aaj bhi Jaggu Babu ya Bada Bajaar.

Baap-dada aaye the kabhi chod UP, Bihar aur Rajasthan,
Phela hae aaj Chitpur se Alipur tak hamara niwas sthaan.

My Calcutta

I'm the 'bodo sahib' in the corner office, somewhere in Dalhousie,
Earl Grey and a tee off get my day started at RCGC.

The 'who's who' gathers for my galas at my bungalow,
Where liveried bearers with potent servings help the conversations flow.

Hung on my walls is an MBBS or a Bar-at-Law from London,
You'll often catch me say, 'My pleasure' or 'I beg your pardon!'

Our City of Joy

Where we love our phuchkas, muri, sandesh and roll,
Where we cheer at Eden for every ball.

Where we are perennially inspired by Kishore, Tagore and Ray,
Where bags get packed for Darjeeling every May.

Where Pujo is the season for Maa Durga, bonhomie and shopping,
Where the feet never tire of pandal hopping.

Where we celebrate joys that are everyday and simple,
Where the spirit remains infectiously intellectual.

To our dear City of Joy—incorrigible, idiosyncratic and lovable!

About the Author

A student of Arts with a Master's degree in International Relations, Supriya Newar has clocked twenty years of keen professional involvement in the world of Brand and Communications.

She has had the privilege of working with significant Indian as well as global brands, leading and training teams and has been writing for noted publications with several hundred articles to her name. She has also conceptualised, curated and authored noteworthy coffee table books.

Born and brought up in Calcutta, she is an aficionado of Indian classical as well as folk music besides being an avid bookworm and a traveller. She's also a Visiting Lecturer at various institutes of repute and serves as a Non-Executive Director on the Board of Linc Pens.

She may be reached at:
Email: connect@supriyanewar.com
Facebook: https://www.facebook.com/supriya.newar
Instagram: @supriyanewar
Web: www.supriyanewar.com